WILDLIFERS

# THE AFRICAN ELEPHANT

Melissa Kim

Illustrated by
Ann Strugnell

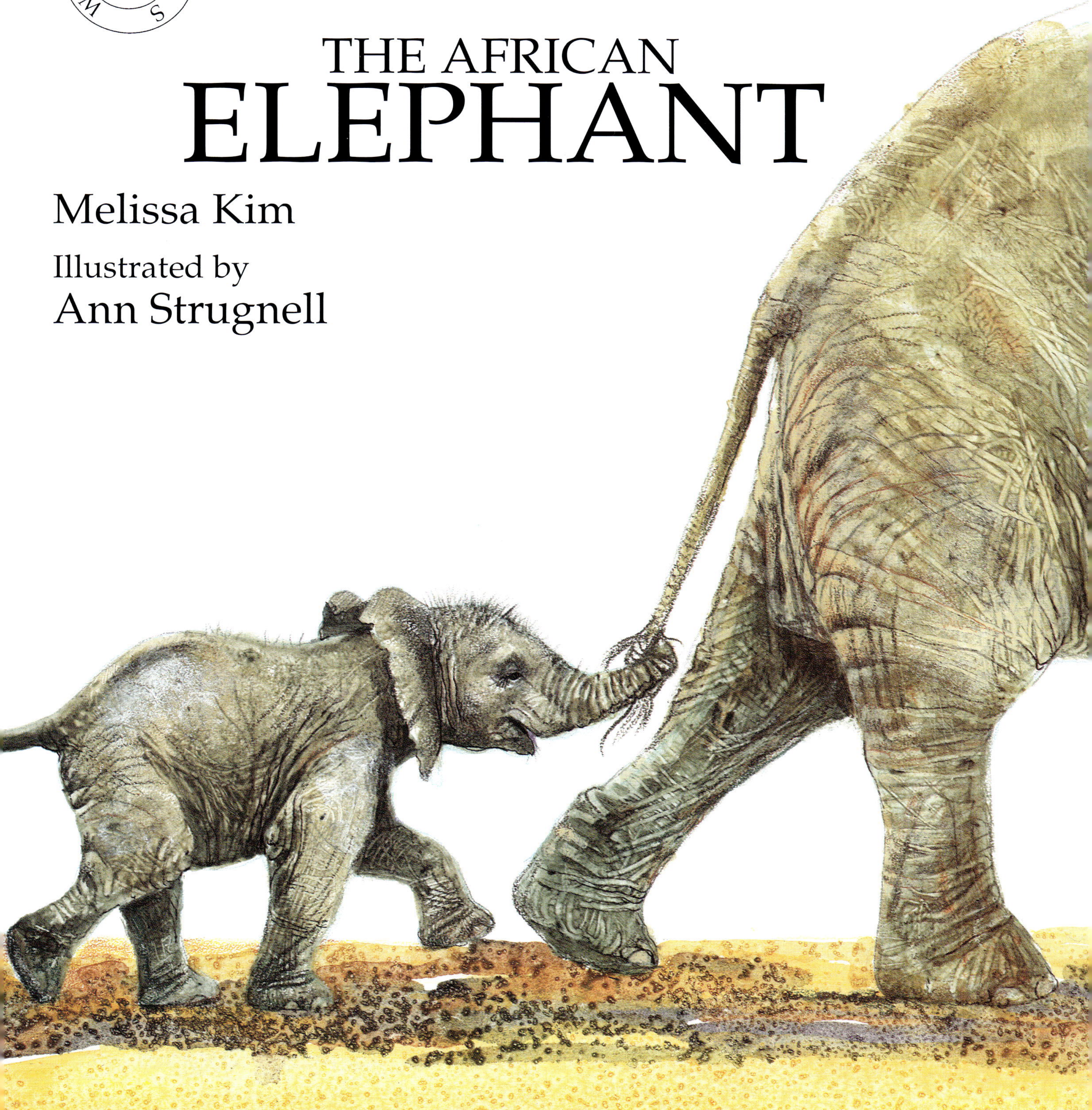

**Hutchinson**
London Sydney Auckland Johannesburg

First published in 1995
1 3 5 7 9 10 8 6 4 2


First published in the United Kingdom in 1995 by
Hutchinson Children's Books
Random House UK Limited
20 Vauxhall Bridge Road
London SW1V 2SA

Random House Australia (Pty) Limited
20 Alfred Street, Milsons Point, Sydney
New South Wales 2061, Australia

Random House New Zealand Limited
18 Poland Street, Glenfield
Auckland 10, New Zealand

Random House South Africa (Pty) Limited
PO Box 337, Bergvlei, South Africa

Random House UK Limited Reg. No. 954009

Conceived, edited, designed, and produced by Signpost Books, Ltd.
25 Eden Drive, Headington, Oxford, England OX3 0AB

Editor: Dorothy Wood
Designer: Krystyna Hewitt

A CIP catalogue record for this book
is available from the British Library

ISBN 0 09 176504 8

Printed in Hong Kong

# SAY NO TO IVORY!

On one side of the world, a woman wears an ivory bracelet while playing a grand piano that has ivory keys, and her husband plays a game that uses ivory billiard balls. On the other side of the world, a huge, majestic elephant lies dying on the dusty ground, shot by an automatic rifle, its ivory tusks ripped out.

**Should this be happening?**
You can discover lots of information about the African elephant, the threats to its survival, and the ways in which you can help save the largest living land animal on earth. If you care about animals in danger, you automatically become a Wildlifer, people who share a common concern for animals and want to make the world a better place for all of us.

# The elephant family

Millions of years ago, huge shaggy beasts with strong legs and long noses roamed almost every corner of the earth. As many as 163 species made up this order of *proboscideans* (pro-buh-SID-e-uns). The word *proboscis* (pro-BOS-kis) means trunk. Some species lived just after the time of the dinosaurs. These animals are the ancestors of the modern-day elephant. They had long snouts with very short tusks, and we have given them odd names like *gomphotheres* and *mammuts*. As time passed, they changed and adapted—their trunks grew longer and their tusks became bigger, and they became mastodons and woolly mammoths.

Today, all of these magnificent creatures are extinct. Only two of their descendants have survived the tough journey of evolution: the *African elephant* and the *Asian elephant*. They are the largest and strongest animals that live on land. Now the elephants are threatened, not by evolution, but by man.

**FACT FILE**

Like elephants, we are mammals too. That means we are warm-blooded, produce milk to feed our young, and have hair on our bodies.

# African or Asian?

An elephant's trunk pokes through the bushes, groping and grasping for some leaves or fruit. The two bumps, or 'fingers', at the end of its trunk pinch off leaves to eat. Its trunk is floppy and flexible. Just looking at the trunk can tell you what kind of elephant it is and which continent you are on.

There are two main types of elephants in the world—the African and the Asian. There are three different families of Asian elephants. They are named after where they live. The three Asian elephant families are the mainland Asian elephant, the Sri Lankan elephant, and the Sumatran elephant. There are two families of African elephants: forest elephants and bush (also called savannah) elephants.

The bush elephant is the largest of all. It can live almost anywhere, from the open plains and grasslands to forest, marshes or mountains. The forest elephant prefers to hide in the thick forests of central and western Africa. Not much is known about this animal. We do know that it has smaller ears and straighter tusks than its bush relative. All African elephants have two 'fingers' or bumps at the end of their flexible trunks, unlike Asian elephants, which have only one 'finger'.

**FACT FILE**

Rare sightings of a very small elephant once led people to believe there was a pygmy elephant living deep in the dense, dark forest of the Congo. But now scientists say these are forest elephants, whose tusks grow so fast that even young elephants can have large tusks and can be mistaken for tiny adults.

**FACT FILE**

Can you tell who's who here? African elephants and Asian elephants are very different. Read the list of differences below and decide which elephant couple is African and which is Asian.

AFRICAN
* Bigger
* Larger ears
* Curved back
* Wrinkled skin
* Flat head
* Belly slopes down from front to back
* Both males and females have tusks
* Highest point is the shoulder
* Two 'fingers' at tip of trunk

ASIAN
* Smaller
* Smaller ears
* Flat back
* Smoother skin
* Bulges in head
* Belly sags in the middle
* Usually only males have tusks
* Highest point is the top of the head
* One 'finger' at tip of trunk

# Characteristics of the African elephant

**EARS**
The African elephant's ear acts as a giant fan, flapping to cool the elephant when there is no wind. The hotter the elephant's home, the larger its ears. Ears are like fingerprints, full of distinct veins, notches, and tears. Scientists use the ears to identify individual elephants.

**TUSKS**
Tusks are long teeth. They grow about 17 cm each year. Tusks don't have an enamel coatingas human teeth do. They are made of pure ivory. Tusks also have nerves, so elephants can feel pain in them. Tusks are used to dig for water, to move trees out of the way, and to strip bark off trees. Elephants sometimes use their tusks as weapons. Tusks also serve as useful resting places for heavy trunks.

**TRUNK**
The trunk is essential to an elephant's life. Elephants breathe through their trunks, drink water, collect and carry food to their mouths, throw dust on their bodies, splash mud and water, smell and touch things, make sounds, carry things, and, if need be, use their trunks as weapons. The trunk is so flexible that an elephant can use it to pick up a small coin. There are no bones in the trunk, just muscles, blood vessels, tissues, hair, and skin. It may have as many as 50,000 muscles (although no one knows for sure).

**TEETH**
An elephant has 24 teeth and 2 tusks. Our teeth fall out and are replaced once in our lives—an elephant's teeth are replaced six times. Sometimes you can tell an elephant's age by its teeth. New teeth come in behind old teeth and gradually move to the front of the mouth as the old teeth fall apart or drop out.

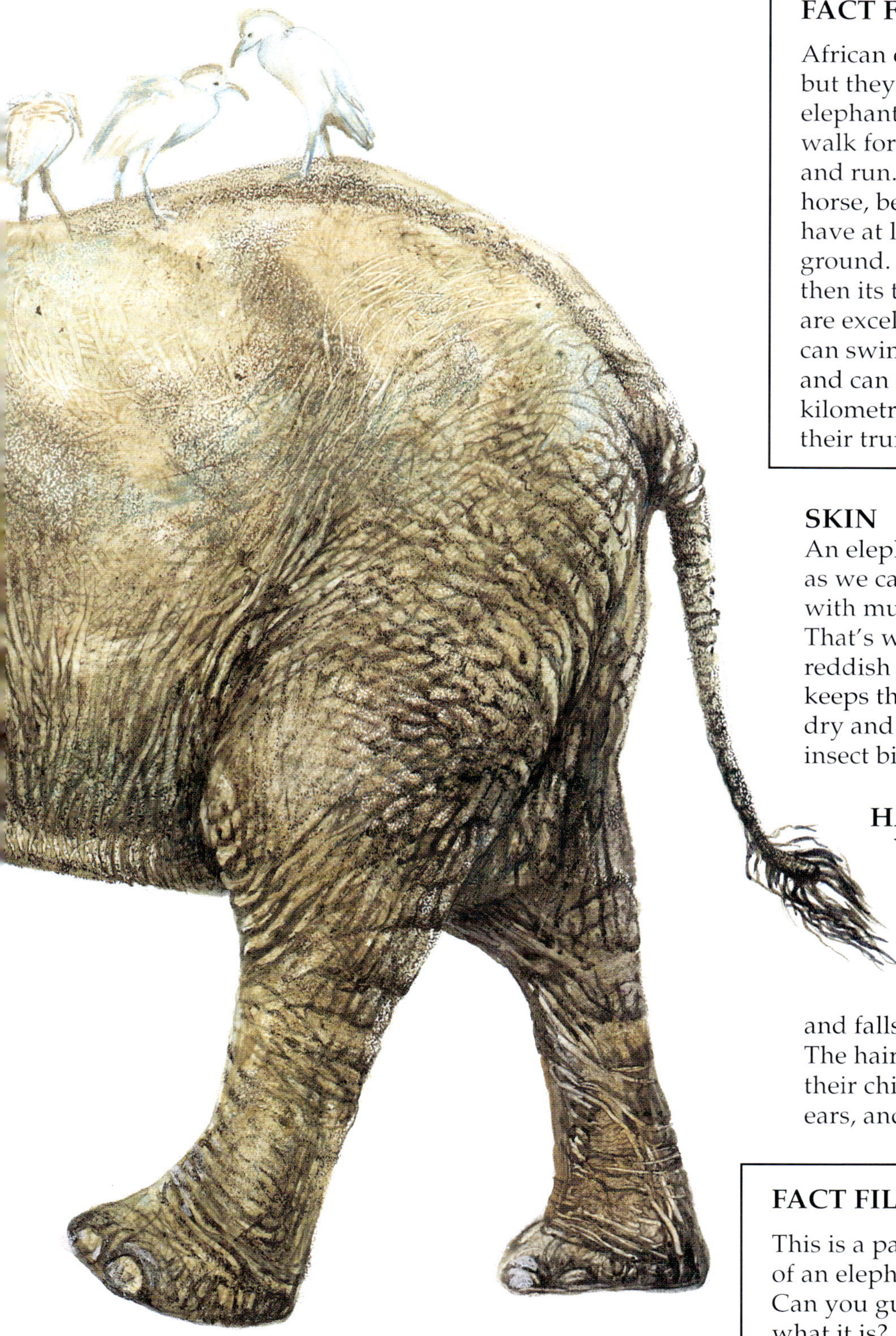

## FACT FILE

African elephants may be big, but they are not clumsy. An elephant can stand on one leg, walk forwards and backwards, and run. It cannot trot like a horse, because it always needs to have at least one foot on the ground. It lifts its two right feet, then its two left feet. Elephants are excellent swimmers—they can swim very long distances and can go as fast as 2.1 kilometres per hour. They use their trunks as snorkels.

## SKIN

An elephant can get sunburnt just as we can, so it covers its skin with mud or dust to protect it. That's why some elephants look reddish in color. The mud also keeps the skin from getting too dry and helps guard against insect bites.

## HAIR

You might not think of elephants as hairy creatures, but baby elephants are covered with reddish-brown hair. The hair gets darker and falls out as they grow older. The hairiest parts of elephants are their chins, around their eyes and ears, and the ends of their tails.

## LEGS

The African elephant's legs have to be very strong to support a lot of weight. Their legs are like columns and can be 'locked' into place, making it more comfortable to stand still for long periods of time.

## FACT FILE

This is a part of an elephant. Can you guess what it is? Where is it located on the elephant's body, and what does it do? The answer is on page 32.

# How big is big?

When an African elephant calf is born, it weighs about 120 kg and is about 85 cm tall at the shoulder.

Elephants continue to grow all their lives. By the time an elephant is ten years old, it weighs between 900 kg and 1,360 kg and is about 2 m tall. An adult elephant weighs between 2,700 kg and 6,000 kg, and is about 3–4 m tall. The females are smaller than the males.

What do these figures really mean?

One large African male elephant weighs as much as…

12 large horses

80 people

48,000 regular hamburgers

1500 cats

6 cars

If the whole elephant is big and heavy, so are each of its body parts. The African elephant has a huge heart that weighs between 11 and 21 kg. Compare that to your own weight. An elephant's ear can weigh 80 kg, as much as an average adult man weighs. And just one of its teeth can weigh 5 kg.

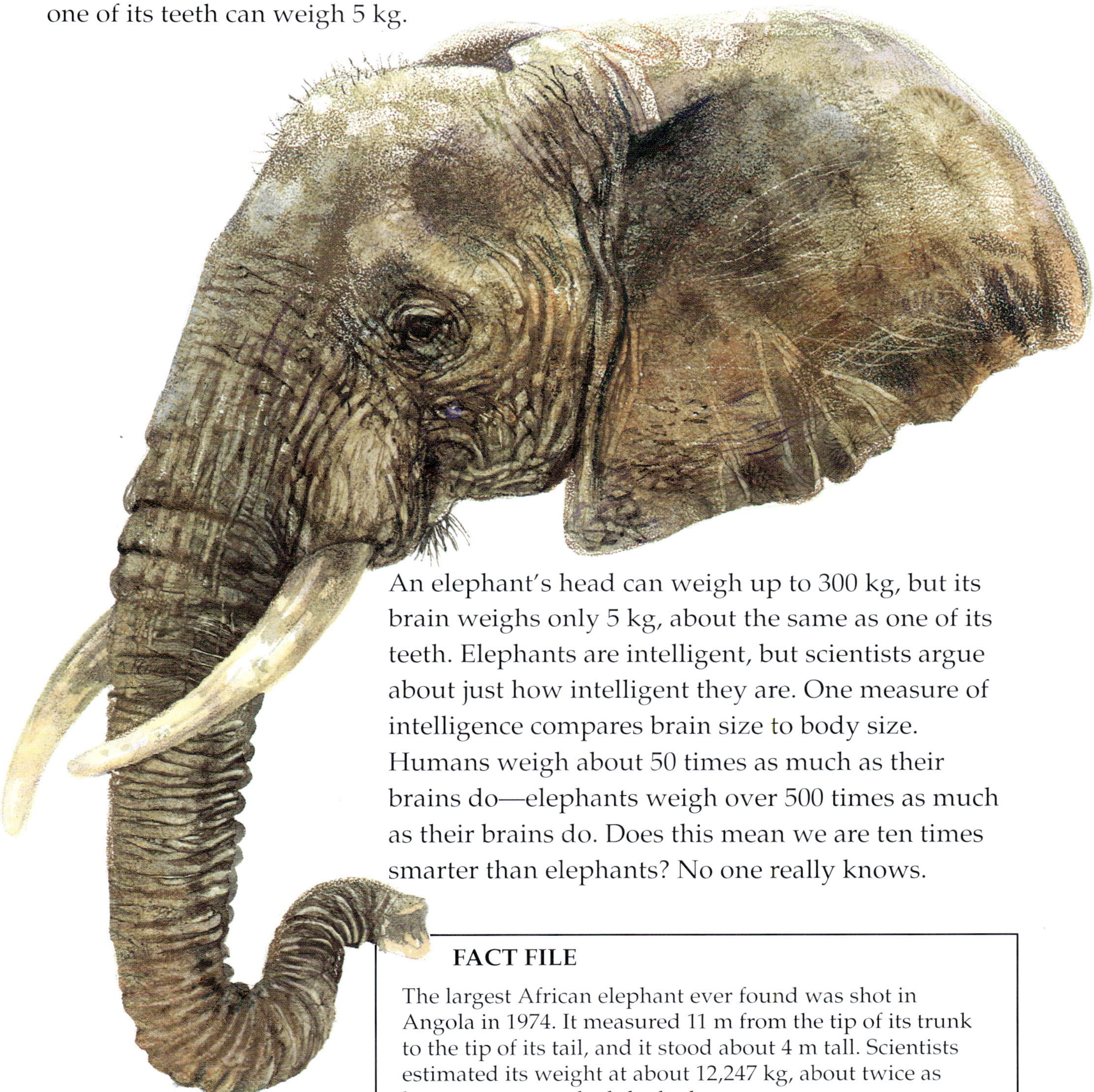

An elephant's head can weigh up to 300 kg, but its brain weighs only 5 kg, about the same as one of its teeth. Elephants are intelligent, but scientists argue about just how intelligent they are. One measure of intelligence compares brain size to body size. Humans weigh about 50 times as much as their brains do—elephants weigh over 500 times as much as their brains do. Does this mean we are ten times smarter than elephants? No one really knows.

**FACT FILE**

The largest African elephant ever found was shot in Angola in 1974. It measured 11 m from the tip of its trunk to the tip of its tail, and it stood about 4 m tall. Scientists estimated its weight at about 12,247 kg, about twice as heavy as a normal adult elephant.

# Where do African elephants live?

Would you be as happy in the desert as in the mountains? Would you feel at home both in a city and in the countryside? Most people and animals have a preferred habitat, or place to live. But African elephants, especially bush elephants, can adapt to and live in a wide variety of places. Bush elephants live in almost every country in Africa that is south or west of the Sahara desert. They are not territorial and will share their home areas with other elephants. In the rainy season, they tend to spread out and live in the open savannahs, or grassland areas. In the dry season, they gather at the few watering holes they can find.

The forest elephant is not quite as adaptable as the bush elephant. It lives in thick forests near the equator in central and western Africa. It will occasionally wander into areas that are between forest and grassland and mingle with the bush elephant.

African elephants are sometimes found in the most unexpected places. Some live in one of the harshest environments in all of Africa—the Namib Desert in Namibia, which has less than 15 cm of rain a year. Very few living things can survive there. But elephants can dig water holes and reach higher for food than any other animal. You may also find elephants underground. An elephant needs salt. It will dig for salt by creating a cave or by widening an existing cave, often in the side of a cliff or the wall of a steep valley. A whole family of elephants can disappear into a hole in the ground, looking for a good salt lick.

**FACT FILE**

Zaire is the country that appears to have the most African elephants, with an estimated population of 90,000. Scientists estimate that there are about 609,000 elephants living in Africa, although it is impossible to determine the exact number. There are about 795,000,000 people living in Africa.

**FACT FILE**

Here's a challenge to your knowledge of geography. Elephants live in the 36 African countries named on this map, but the countries' names have been scrambled. Unscramble the letters to find out the names of the elephants' homes. The answers are on page 32.

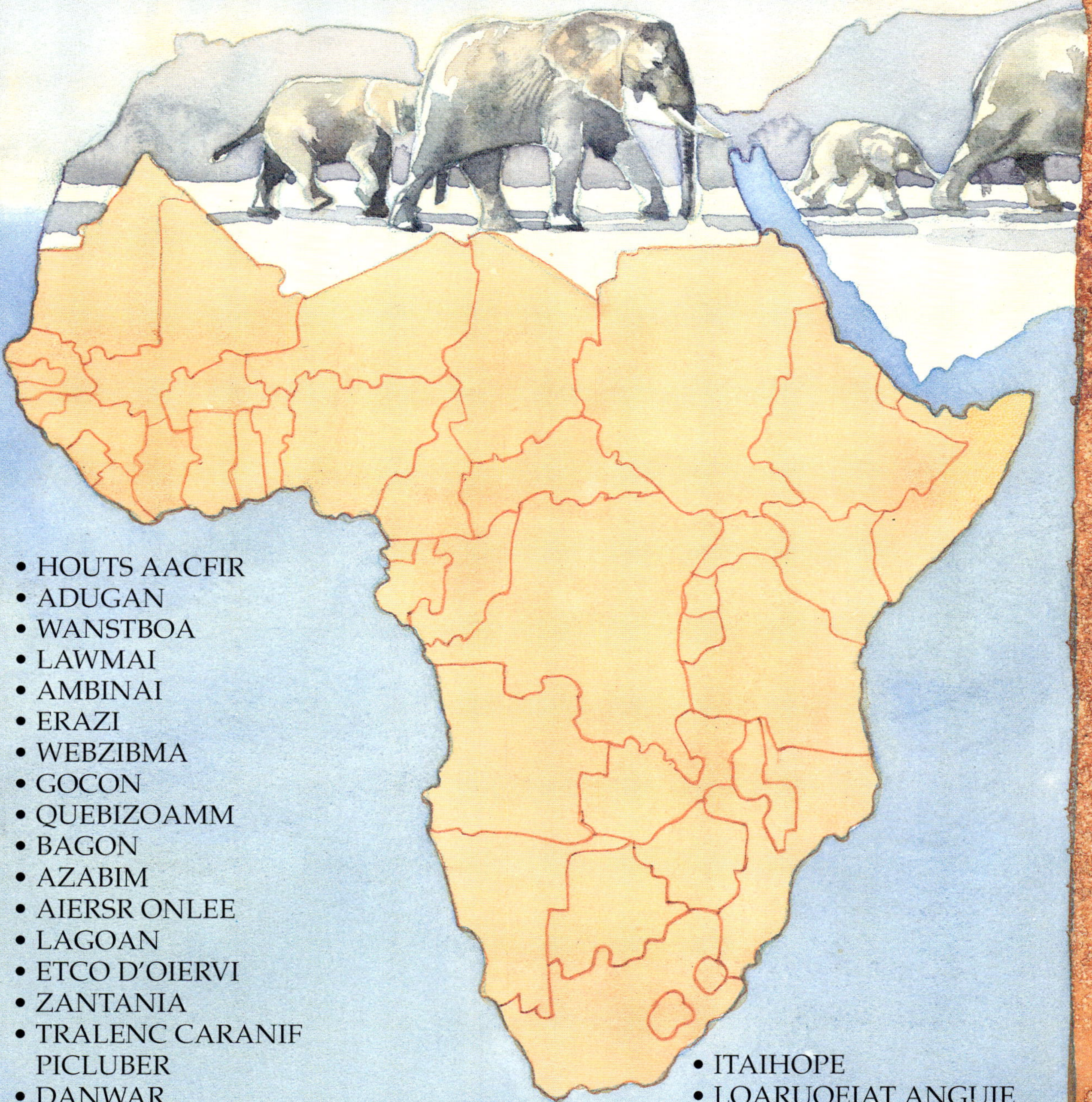

- HOUTS AACFIR
- ADUGAN
- WANSTBOA
- LAWMAI
- AMBINAI
- ERAZI
- WEBZIBMA
- GOCON
- QUEBIZOAMM
- BAGON
- AZABIM
- AIERSR ONLEE
- LAGOAN
- ETCO D'OIERVI
- ZANTANIA
- TRALENC CARANIF PICLUBER
- DANWAR
- YAKNE
- ONCEMARO
- IANURATMIA
- GOOT
- GLEENAS
- SNAUD
- INDRBUU
- ANGUIE
- DACH
- GREIN
- GANUIE-SAUSBI
- AILBERI
- ITAIHOPE
- LOARUQEIAT ANGUIE
- MILAOSA
- KRABINU SOFA
- LIAM
- AINGERI
- INBEN
- AHGAN

# What do elephants eat?

An acacia tree sags limply near a stream, its bark peeled, its branches broken and bearing very few leaves. It hasn't been hit by lightning—the damage has been caused by an elephant having a meal. The acacia tree is one of the elephant's favourite foods, and the elephant eats almost every part of it—the roots, bark, leaves, twigs, thorns, branches, and pods.

African elephants are herbivores, or plant eaters. They eat more than 80 different kinds of trees and plants. They also enjoy grasses. They are called *browsers* because they can eat vegetation that grows above the ground. They eat just about anything and everything. In fact, they destroy many shrubs and trees, shoving over a tree just to get at the leaves. Animals that have such a dramatic impact on their environment just by feeding are called *mega-herbivores*. Other mega-herbivores are rhinos, hippos, and giraffes.

Because plants don't contain a great deal of nutrients or protein, an elephant has to eat a lot in order to get what it needs. An average adult male eats between 100 and 300 kg during an average day. It takes a long time to gather and eat that much food. Some elephant watchers say the animals spend between sixteen and eighteen hours a day eating.

African elephants usually have three 'meals' a day. They have long feeding sessions at night and in the very early morning. They feed again for a short time around noon, but most animals want to avoid the midday heat. Then an elephant will rest or nap standing up. Elephants only lie down to sleep in the middle of the night, and then for only a few hours.

## FACT FILE

These are a few of the African elephant's favourite foods. See if you can match the description with the illustration.

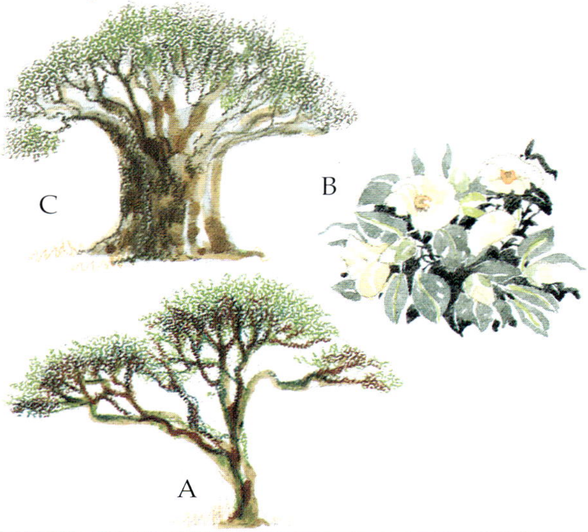


The acacia tree is a tall shade tree, flat on top, with a long trunk and twisted thorny branches. It has pods and tiny white, yellow, and orange flowers.

The gardenia tree or shrub bears a bitter, hard fruit that is bigger than a tennis ball. It has fragrant waxy white or yellow flowers, and dark glossy leaves.

The baobab tree has a very thick trunk, as much as 9 m in circumference. Its long, widespread branches look more like roots. Many people say it looks as if it is upside down. It has big white flowers and gourd-like fruit.

The answers are on page 32.

## FACT FILE

How does your daily routine compare with that of an elephant? An African elephant spends about sixteen to eighteen hours a day finding and eating food. How many hours of the day do you spend gathering, preparing, and eating food (including shopping time and cleanup time)? Make up your own chart, writing down everything you do in a typical day, and figure out how much time you spend on food.

| | DAILY ACTIVITIES | FOOD-RELATED ACTIVITIES | TIME SPENT ON FOOD |
|---|---|---|---|
| 7 - 8am | | | |
| 8 - 9am | | | |
| 9 - 10am | | | |
| 10 - 11am | | | |
| 11 - 12am | | | |
| 12 - 1pm | | | |
| 1 - 2pm | | | |
| 2 - 3pm | | | |
| 3 - 4pm | | | |
| 4 - 5pm | | | |
| 5 - 6pm | | | |
| 6 - 7pm | | | |
| 7 - 8pm | | | |
| 8 - 9pm | | | |
| 9 - 10pm | | | |
| 10 - 11pm | | | |
| 11 - 12pm | | | |
| | | | Total time spent |

How many hours a day do you spend on food? Is it more or less than the African elephant?

# Do elephants have families?

Picture a group of African elephants walking along, eating, or playing. There are about nine or ten elephants in the group, and most of them are related. There are a mother, daughters, sons, aunts, cousins, and nieces. All are members of the very important elephant family. Elephants have very close families and find it difficult to survive without them.

The group here is about average in size, although some families have as few as five members while others have as many as twenty. There is one large elephant that seems to be in charge. When she moves, everyone else follows. This elephant is the *matriarch*, the female in charge of the family unit. The matriarch decides when and where the family will travel. As the oldest member of the family, she has a lifetime of experience that will keep the family healthy and safe.

To one side are two more females, about the same age, maybe 30 or 40 years old, and probably sisters. The matriarch has two daughters, 18 or 20 years old. There is a young male, about 10 years old, hanging

**FACT FILE**

Male elephants leave the family when they are between 10 and 14 years old. Some live the rest of their lives more or less alone, attaching themselves to families now and then. Some form *bachelor herds*, joining together with other young males.

Here is an example of a typical elephant family tree, headed by a matriarch named Lily. Horizontal lines connecting elephants mean they are brothers or sisters. Vertical lines mean they are children or parents. Make your own family tree. Start with your grandparents and draw three generations. How does your family tree differ from this one?

around the edge of the group. There are also a few calves, peeking out from between the mother's or aunt's or grandmother's legs. Except for the males, which will leave to explore the world on their own, this group will remain a family unit for life. Unlike humans, African elephants do not pair up and form 'couples'. Families have mostly female members. They travel together, eat and sleep together, and search for food and water together. They care for members who are sick or injured and protect each other in times of danger. They probably belong to a larger herd, made up of three or four other family units. This herd is called a *bond group* or a *kinship group* and can be very large. They stay in touch with their group, never straying too far out of earshot. They may spend a few days apart, then drift back together.

When elephant groups gather together, it's time for a celebration! Elephants use elaborate ceremonies to greet each other. They trumpet, bellow, rumble, nudge and bump one another, and sniff each other all over with their trunks.

# An elephant childhood

A large African elephant stands patiently, ears flapping, trunk swaying. Hiding underneath her is a small grey shape with a small trunk and a pair of curious eyes. It's a baby elephant, standing under its mother's belly for shade and protection.

At birth, a baby African elephant weighs about 120 kg and measures about 85 cm at the shoulder. In the same way as humans, an elephant is born with very little knowledge of the world, and how to survive and behave in it. For one thing, it cannot see very well and has to be taught almost everything, even how to use its trunk. At first, a baby elephant can't control its long wobbly nose and trips on it or sucks on it, just as human babies suck their thumbs. But soon it can pick up twigs and, in a few months, it will try to feed itself blades of grass.

Babies are the pride and joy of every elephant family. Each family member takes part in the baby's learning and care. Young females are especially interested in babies and become aunts, or *allmothers*, to them. They wake them up when it's time to travel, help them if they get stuck in the mud, and stand over them while they sleep. These aunts are very helpful to a busy learning how to become mothers themselves.

At the age of nine months a baby can eat grass and plants, but it stays dependent on its mother's milk for two to three years. During its childhood, an elephant learns a lot by playing. Males learn how to spar, fight, push, and shove. Females play games with lots of running and chasing. As they grow older, females grow closer to the

**FACT FILE**

Female elephants have one baby about every four to six years. They have the longest *gestation period* (the time it takes a baby to grow inside its mother) of all mammals. It takes between eighteen and twenty-two months, compared to nine months for humans. One female will have from five to as many as twelve babies in her lifetime.

family, while males grow more independent. Females become adults in nine or ten years; males mature a few years later. Females will then have babies of their own, and males will leave the herd to live on their own and search for females with which to mate.

**FACT FILE**

Elephants usually live to be between 50 and 70 years old. Some people believe the oldest elephant ever known was an Asian elephant named Raja, who was reported to be 82 years old when he died.

# Can elephants communicate?

A group of African elephants stand in the hot plains. Suddenly, one lifts its head. The others look up too. The matriarch begins to walk off in one direction and the rest follow. Miles away, another group of elephants drink and bathe in a water hole. An hour later, the first group appear at the water hole, and the second group greet them with trumpets and rumbles. How did the first group know where to go? Scientists now realize that elephants communicate by *infrasound*—a sound that is very low in pitch, so low that humans cannot hear it. Infrasound travels well over large areas and can carry through grasslands or woodlands. It is the perfect way for bond groups to stay in touch. They can explore large areas for food and water, females can signal when they are ready to mate, and they can alert each other to danger.

Elephants also communicate with other sounds. A low rumble might mean 'Let's go', or a high trumpet might mean 'I want to play'. Researchers have identified about thirty 'phrases' in elephants' language. Elephants use touch, chemical signals, smell and visual displays to communicate as well.

**FACT FILE**

Elephants use much the same sort of body language as humans do. Here are some elephant body positions and what scientists think they might mean. There are also some human body positions. What do you think they mean?

Answers on p. 32.

# How intelligent are elephants?

Think of all the things elephants can do: they can pick up a branch and use it to scratch their backs; or move a log at the command of a trainer; or remember a good path to a water hole; or even chew up bark to make a plug for a water hole. Are these signs of intelligence? It is hard to define intelligence, but being able to make and use tools is usually a good sign of it. The ability to learn and remember things is another mark of intelligence. Elephants can do both.

Elephants can also be trained. In fact, man has been using elephants for almost 4,000 years. They were once used in battles—in groups called the *elephantry*—to carry soldiers and to scare the enemy. Elephants have been trained to transport and move heavy loads, carry tourists, and lead religious ceremonies. It has usually been the Asian elephant which has been trained to serve man, while the African elephant has resisted being tamed. But some scientists believe that the African elephant can also be trained, and one training project in Zaire has proved that these scientists are correct. The African elephants there have been trained to move objects and to carry tourists on safari.

**FACT FILE**

One of the most curious things about elephants is what happens when an elephant dies. The others in the group will try to pick it up. They may throw dust and leaves on it and stand over the dead animal for hours. If they come across the body of a dead elephant they will smell and touch the body all over. Elephants can also recognize the body of a dead relative. There is a popular, but unproven, idea that there are elephant graveyards, special places where elephants go to die.

**FACT FILE**

Elephants have been performing in western zoos and circuses since at least the mid-1800s. It is now very difficult to import elephants, but there are at least 1,200 Asian and 700 African elephants in zoos, circuses, and parks worldwide.

# How important are elephants?

Architect, bulldozer, gardener, destroyer—the African elephant has been called all of these things. That is because it is one of the few animals that can shape its environment. It doesn't just have an effect on its home. It creates and destroys it—and this can have both good and bad results.

These are some of the ways in which African elephants change their habitat, and the results of what they do.

Elephants strip trees of their bark and leaves. They destroy trees and turn woodland into grassland.

**Good:** Animals that live in grasslands have new homes.
**Bad:** Animals that live in woodlands have less food and fewer places to live.

**FACT FILE**

An animal that can shape its environment is called a *keystone species.* Can you think of other keystone species? Who can create or destroy homes? Who can help or hurt others?

In the rainforest or thick forest, elephants create clearings by eating and trampling thick vegetation.

**Good:** This allows the sun to enter the forest, which helps new plants to grow. Forest animals such as gorillas and small deer come to feed in the clearings.
**Bad:** Elephants destroy some plant and animal species.

Elephants create paths to water holes by trampling down vegetation. They also create or enlarge some water holes by digging with their tusks.

**Good:** This helps all the animals find water.
**Bad:** Some vegetation is destroyed.

Elephants dig or enlarge caves in search of salt.

**Good:** This allows other animals to find salt and shelter too.
**Bad:** If they dig too much, elephants can cause erosion and the caves will collapse.

Elephants eat fruit and leave the seeds of the fruit behind in their dung. Their rich manure helps the seeds to grow. By spreading seeds, they have earned the nickname 'gardener'.

**Good:** They help trees and plants to spread their seeds and create new generations.
**Bad:** None known.

Elephants disturb birds, reptiles, and tiny insects as they trample through the tall grass.

**Good:** Birds follow the elephants and eat the insects the elephants turn up.
**Bad:** Some insects and reptiles are trampled by the elephants.

Do you think the good things outweigh the bad? For every habitat, the key to survival is balance. While every species plays its part, it is clear that the elephant plays a special role in keeping things balanced. Without the elephant, many species would die and the face of Africa would change completely.

# Is the elephant endangered?

Both the African elephant and the Asian elephant are endangered species. This means there is a very real danger that they could become extinct. Why is the elephant endangered? Like many other animals, the elephant has lost some of its homeland to man. The human population of Africa increases every year, and people need land in order to live and grow food. But the main reason the African elephants are endangered is that people kill them.

In the ten years between 1979 and 1989, according to one researcher, the elephant population of Africa went from 1,300,000 to 609,000. In ten years, half of the entire elephant population died.

**FACT FILE**
A tusk has many nerves and tissues. If a tusk is removed from an elephant that is alive, it causes the elephant enormous pain and creates a high risk of infection. An elephant without tusks would find it hard to survive.

African elephants are killed for their tusks, which are the world's best source of ivory. They are not too soft or too hard and are easy to carve into ornaments and jewellery. Ever since Europeans came to Africa, elephants have been hunted for their ivory tusks. When Great Britain, France, Belgium, and other European nations colonized many African countries, they installed their own governments. In the early part of this century, many of these colonial governments passed laws to control the number of elephants killed.

But in the 1950s and 1960s, many African nations regained their independence, and there was often serious fighting. Many tribes fought each other, and a record number of guns were imported and sold in Africa. Many of the old colonial laws were cast aside. Elephants could now be killed with powerful automatic weapons, and no laws would protect them.

At the same time, the price of ivory began to rise. Ivory became more and more valuable to people. In Japan, particularly, ivory is highly prized. The Japanese use seals made of carved ivory to sign their names. These signature seals are like rubber stamps—the characters are carved into a block of ivory, then the bottom is inked and pressed onto paper. As the demand for these signature seals grew, so did the price of ivory. In the 1950s and 1960s, ivory cost about £1.45 per kg. By 1978, it cost £21.50 per kg, and in 1989, in Japan, it cost £190.00 per kg.

Becoming a poacher, a hunter of illegal products, was one way to become rich very quickly. No one paid any attention to the laws that banned the sale or use of ivory.

And so elephants died in their thousands. As large adult elephants with big tusks were killed, many babies were left on their own. Without their families to support them and teach them, they too died or failed to mate. And as the adult population declined, poachers began killing younger elephants too.

**FACT FILE**

Ivory comes from elephants, narwhal whales, mammoths, and walruses. It is used to make the products below. Can we find substitutes for them? Can we live without them?

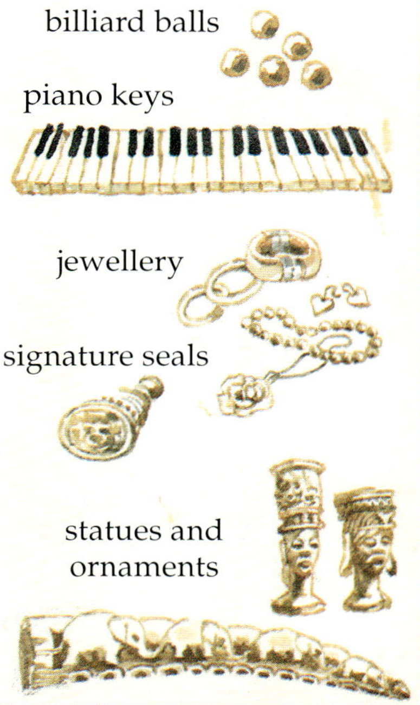

# Is the elephant protected?

Finally, the international community heard the cries of the African elephants and of the scientists who had been warning everyone for years of the elephant's shaky future. In 1989, the African elephant became an officially endangered species. In January 1990, all international trade in elephants and parts of elephants (like ivory) became illegal under a United Nations (UN) ban. The ban is called the Convention for International Trade in Endangered Species, or CITES. African elephants received a lot of attention and the public showed its support. The market for ivory all but disappeared. Even the famous piano maker, Steinway, announced it would no longer use ivory to make its piano keys. Several African governments spent money on anti-poaching groups, and some burned huge piles of illegally hunted ivory. All of these actions helped make ivory traders and poachers realize the ban was serious.

Now the price of ivory has dropped and poaching has slowed down. Many ivory factories in India, Hong Kong, and China have closed, but the CITES ban doesn't entirely protect elephants. It only bans the sale of ivory across international borders and for commercial purposes. Ivory can still be sold within a country. African elephants are still killed for sport, and hunters can still take their trophies home with them. Some countries in southern Africa oppose the CITES ban. In their countries, they say, the elephant populations are healthy and even increasing. They want to be able to sell ivory legally to raise money. The CITES ban allows these countries to

**FACT FILE**

The Asian elephant is even more endangered than the African elephant, with a population of 34,500–44,000. It is endangered mainly because it has nowhere to live. In India, the elephant has lost its habitat to coffee and tea plantations, mining projects, human settlements, and hydro-electric projects. It has not been subjected to as much poaching because only the male has tusks, and these tusks are smaller than those of the African elephant. The Asian elephant became an endangered species protected by CITES in 1977.

**FACT FILE**

Although the big game hunters of Africa are now a part of its past, there are still people who go to Africa to kill wild animals. In Zimbabwe, the Campfire programme allows tourists to kill a certain number of African elephants every year in their game parks. The tourists pay £3,000 or more for their trophies—the tusks, heads, or skins. The money goes to local projects and the people who live near the game parks. The government says there are more than enough elephants, and the Campfire programme raises money to keep the parks running and the local people happy. Would you want an elephant trophy in your home? Or would you ban this kind of programme?

ask for a review every two years. If the elephant population seems stable, some ivory trade may be allowed. It is only the possibility that the ivory trade may one day be allowed that has kept poachers' hopes alive.

Some reports claim that there is still a lot of poaching and ivory smuggling in southern Africa and that poachers are collecting ivory, waiting and hoping for the ban to be lifted. Some countries in southern Africa tried to have the ban lifted in 1992, claiming they would control the ivory trade legally. They were voted down, but they will surely try again. Of course, not all countries in the world belong to the United Nations, and not all UN members are CITES members. There is no way to prevent the ivory trade in countries that are not part of CITES.

# What does the future hold for the elephant?

Elephants will only be safe if both governments and people help them. The CITES ban is very important to their survival, but the only way to safeguard the future of elephants is to erase the need for ivory altogether. As long as people want ivory, elephants will die. Researchers have many different ideas about how to help elephants in Africa. Some of these ideas will work together, but others will work against each other. Not everybody agrees about what to do next. These are some of the ideas.

**Tourism and parks:** Tourism is one good way to help African wildlife. Money from tourists could be used to establish or maintain reserves or parks where animals would be safe from poachers and from losing their homes.

**Captive breeding:** Some scientists want to keep elephants in zoos and parks to breed them. If the population in the wild gets too low, zoo-born animals could be released into the wild. But there has been little success breeding elephants in zoos.

**Culling:** This is the humane killing of elephants in places where the population is high in order to maintain the ecological balance. The meat, ivory, and skins would be sold.

**Domestication:** Some scientists are training African elephants so that they can perform useful tasks. People could then use them to carry objects or move large trees. Tourists could even ride on the backs of domesticated elephants.

**Game ranches:** Some farmers are trying to raise native animals like elephants, buffalo, zebras, wildebeest, impalas, rhinos, and hippos instead of cattle. They think it will be more natural and better for the land in the long run. They can sell the meat and take in tourists and hunters.

**Sport hunting:** People will still pay large sums of money to shoot elephants for fun. The money could go to help local populations.

# What can we do to help?

You might think you can't do much on your own for African elephants. But any effort you make helps them, and that helps African wildlife in general. Here are some things you can do.

**Don't buy ivory.** You can still find ivory for sale, both at home and in other countries. Don't buy it! If you find a store selling ivory, ask them to stop.

**Support wildlife conservation groups.** Write letters of support and find out from them what you can do to help.

**Educate others.** Talk to other people about what you have learned. Create respect for animals and nature.

Any action you take to help an endangered animal shows that you care about the world. And that makes you a true Wildlifer.

Here are the addresses of some organizations that help elephants. Write to them for more information.

The Born Free Foundation
Coldharbour
Dorking, Surrey
RH5 6HA

The African Ele-fund
PO Box 308
Bristol BS99 7LQ

Enviromental Investigation Agency
208-209 Upper Street
London N1 1RL

World Wide Fund for Nature
11-13 Ockford Road
Godalming, Surrey, GU 4PY

# A race for water

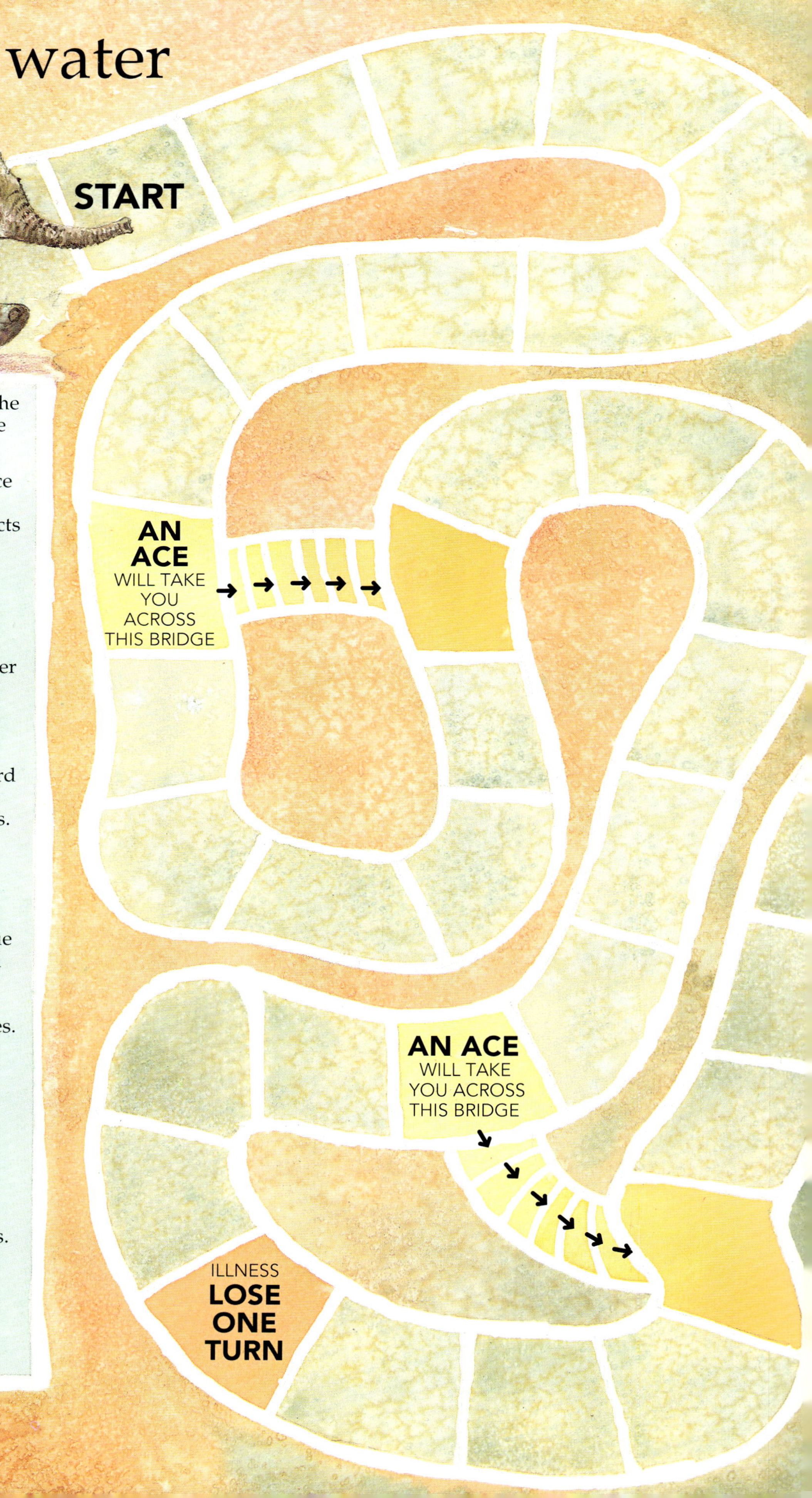


This is a game for two players. The goal is to get your elephant to the watering hole first.

Each player needs one game piece (to represent one elephant). The pieces can be any flat, small objects that fit into the squares on the board, such as a coin, button or stone. You also need a pack of playing cards.

TO PLAY

- Deal out ten cards to each player and leave the remaining cards face down in a pile.
- Flip a coin to decide who goes first, then alternate turns.
- The first player may select a card from either his or her hand or from the top of the pile of cards. If a card is taken from the pile, play that card immediately.

TO MOVE

- Cards 2–10: Move a number of spaces that equals the face value of the card. For example, if you have a 5, move your piece forward 5 spaces.
- Kings: Move backward 5 spaces.
- Queens: Gain an extra turn.
- Jacks: Lose a turn.
- Aces: Jump bridges or move 1 space.

STRATEGY TIPS

- Hold your queens until you really need them.
- If you have an ace, try to move your piece to one of the bridges.
- If you have only low cards in your hand, take a chance and draw from the pile.

The first elephant to reach the watering hole wins!

AN ACE
WILL TAKE YOU ACROSS THIS BRIDGE
POACHER
LOSE 1 TURN
POACHERS
BACK 3 PLACES!
FINISH
THE WATERING HOLE

# Index



# Answers

pages 8–9: It's a nostril. It's at the end of the trunk. Elephants breathe through both their nostrils and their mouths.

pages 12–13: 1. South Africa, 2. Uganda, 3. Botswana, 4. Malawi, 5. Namibia, 6. Zaire, 7. Zimbabwe, 8. Congo, 9. Mozambique, 10. Gabon, 11. Zambia, 12. Sierra Leone, 13. Angola, 14. Côte d'Ivoire, 15. Tanzania, 16. Central African Republic, 17. Rwanda, 18. Kenya, 19. Cameroon, 20. Mauritania, 21. Togo, 22. Senegal, 23. Sudan, 24. Guinea, 25. Chad, 26. Niger, 27. Guinea–Bissau, 28. Liberia, 29. Ethiopia, 30. Equatorial Guinea, 31. Somalia, 32. Burkina Faso, 33. Mali, 34. Nigeria, 35. Benin, 36. Ghana, 37. Burundi.

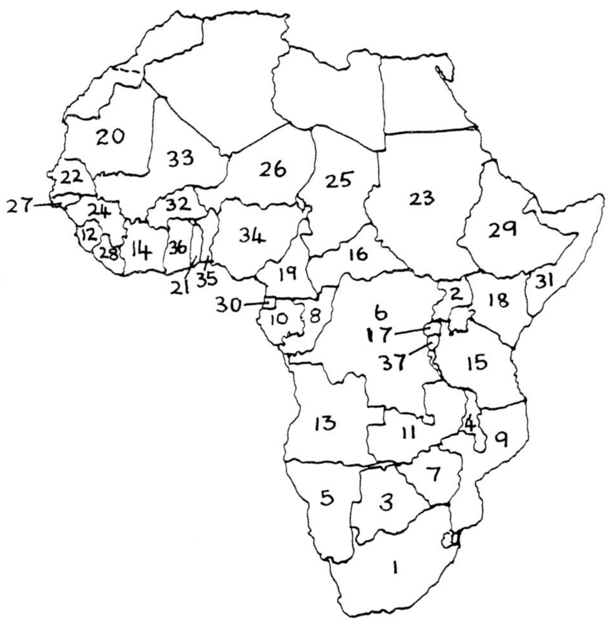


pages 14–15: A—acacia.
B—gardenia
C—baobab

page 20: 1. Warning, 2. Threatening, 3. Attacking, 4. Submitting.